Jeff Stelling

# Chapter 1: Introduction to Robert Jeffrey Stelling

Robert Jeffrey Stelling, born on March 18, 1955, in Hartlepool, England, emerged from humble beginnings to become one of the most recognizable faces in British sports broadcasting. Raised in a council house in Hartlepool, Stelling's formative years were shaped by the industrious spirit of his hometown.

Stelling's educational journey began at Rift House Primary School, where he laid the groundwork for his future endeavors. His thirst for knowledge and passion for sports led him to West Hartlepool Grammar School, where he honed his skills and nurtured his love for journalism.

Following his graduation, Stelling embarked on his professional journey as a journalist at the Hartlepool Mail. For four years, he immersed himself in the world of print media, covering local events and honing his storytelling craft. Little did he know that this early experience would lay the foundation for his illustrious career in broadcasting.

As a young journalist, Stelling displayed a natural flair for communication and a keen eye for detail. His ability to captivate audiences and dissect sporting events earned him recognition within the industry. It wasn't long before his talents caught the attention of radio executives, paving the way for his transition into broadcasting.

Stelling's career trajectory was set in motion with his role as a reporter on Middlesbrough F.C. for Radio Tees in the late 1970s. This marked the beginning of his journey from the written word to the airwaves, where he would soon become a household name.

From his early days at Radio Tees to his later stints at LBC Radio and BBC Radio 2, Stelling's ascent in the world of broadcasting was swift and steady. His passion for sports and gift for engaging storytelling endeared him to audiences across the country, laying the groundwork for a career that would span decades.

In the following chapters, we will delve deeper into Stelling's remarkable journey, exploring the pivotal moments and defining experiences that shaped his life and career. From his iconic tenure as the host of Gillette Soccer Saturday to his philanthropic endeavors and personal triumphs, Robert Jeffrey Stelling's story is one of resilience, dedication, and unwavering passion.

Stelling's transition from print journalism to broadcasting marked a significant turning point in his career. His innate ability to convey the drama and excitement of sporting events through the spoken word propelled him to new heights in the world of media.

After gaining valuable experience as a sports reporter on various radio stations, Stelling seized the opportunity to expand his horizons. His move to London's LBC Radio Sportswatch program in the early 1980s provided him with a platform to showcase his talents on a larger scale. It was here that he honed his skills as a sports presenter, captivating audiences with his dynamic delivery and encyclopedic knowledge of the game.

Stelling's reputation continued to grow as he transitioned to BBC Radio 2's weekend sports program, Sport on 2. Covering prestigious events such as the Los Angeles and Seoul Olympic Games, he cemented his status as a trusted voice in sports broadcasting.

However, it was Stelling's foray into television that would truly catapult him into the spotlight. His tenure as a sports newsreader at TV-am, Channel 4, Eurosport, and British Satellite Broadcasting provided him with invaluable exposure and experience in front of the camera.

In 1992, Stelling made a career-defining move to Sky Sports, where he would spend the next three decades shaping the landscape of sports broadcasting. His versatility as a presenter was on full display as he covered a wide range of sports, including horse racing, greyhound racing, snooker, and darts.

But it was his role as the host of Gillette Soccer Saturday that would solidify Stelling's place in broadcasting history. Since taking the helm in 1994, he transformed the show into a beloved institution, captivating audiences with his wit, charm, and encyclopedic knowledge of the beautiful game.

Throughout his tenure, Stelling became synonymous with Soccer Saturday, earning praise for his exceptional professionalism and unwavering dedication to his craft. His ability to seamlessly navigate the fast-paced world of live sports broadcasting endeared him to viewers and pundits alike, making him a beloved figure in living rooms across the country.

In the following chapters, we will explore Stelling's unparalleled impact on Soccer Saturday and delve into the defining moments of his illustrious career at Sky Sports. From his memorable interactions with pundits to his legendary catchphrases, Robert Jeffrey Stelling's journey into broadcasting is a testament to the power of passion, perseverance, and the enduring magic of live television.

Chapter 2: Journey into Broadcasting

Robert Jeffrey Stelling's journey into broadcasting was a gradual yet remarkable evolution, marked by his transition from print journalism to the dynamic world of radio and television. It was a path paved with determination, passion, and an unwavering commitment to excellence.

Stelling's initial foray into broadcasting began with his role as a reporter on Middlesbrough F.C. for Radio Tees in the late 1970s. This early experience provided him with a firsthand understanding of the intricacies of sports reporting and ignited his passion for sharing the drama of live events with audiences.

Building on his success at Radio Tees, Stelling seized the opportunity to broaden his horizons by venturing into the realm of radio broadcasting. His early roles on LBC Radio and BBC Radio 2 laid the groundwork for his future endeavors, allowing him to refine his skills as a sports presenter and establish himself as a trusted voice in the industry.

At LBC Radio, Stelling showcased his natural charisma and talent for engaging storytelling, captivating listeners with his insightful commentary and infectious enthusiasm for sports. His ability to connect with audiences on a personal level set him apart, earning him a dedicated following and opening doors to new opportunities.

Transitioning to BBC Radio 2, Stelling continued to shine, covering prestigious sporting events such as the Los Angeles and Seoul Olympic Games. His versatility as a broadcaster was evident as he effortlessly navigated between live commentary, analysis, and interviews, earning accolades for his professionalism and passion for the game.

As his reputation grew, Stelling's journey took him to various broadcasting platforms, each contributing to his evolution as a multifaceted media personality. From TV-am to Channel 4, Eurosport, and British Satellite Broadcasting, he left an indelible mark on the landscape of sports broadcasting, showcasing his versatility and adaptability across different mediums.

It was at Sky Sports, however, where Stelling would truly make his mark, solidifying his status as one of the most iconic figures in British sports broadcasting. His tenure at Sky Sports spanned three decades and encompassed a wide range of sports, from horse racing and greyhound racing to snooker and darts.

In the following chapters, we will delve deeper into Stelling's illustrious career at Sky Sports, exploring his legendary tenure as the host of Gillette Soccer Saturday and his enduring impact on the world of sports broadcasting. From his memorable catchphrases to his unparalleled passion for the game, Robert Jeffrey Stelling's journey into broadcasting is a testament to the power of perseverance, dedication, and the relentless pursuit of excellence.

Chapter 3: Sky Sports Career

Robert Jeffrey Stelling's tenure at Sky Sports is synonymous with excellence, innovation, and a deep-rooted passion for sports broadcasting. Over the course of three decades, he carved out a distinguished career, leaving an indelible mark on the network and captivating audiences with his unparalleled charisma and expertise.

Stelling's journey at Sky Sports began in 1992, where he quickly established himself as a versatile presenter with a knack for bringing the excitement of live sports to viewers across the country. His early roles included presenting coverage of a diverse range of sports, from horse racing and greyhound racing to snooker and darts. Through his insightful commentary and engaging presentation style, Stelling endeared himself to audiences and laid the groundwork for his future success.

However, it was Stelling's iconic tenure as the host of Gillette Soccer Saturday that would elevate him to legendary status within the world of sports broadcasting. Since taking the helm in 1994, he transformed the show into a beloved institution, captivating viewers with his wit, charm, and encyclopedic knowledge of the beautiful game.

Week after week, Stelling guided viewers through the highs and lows of the football season, providing live updates, analysis, and commentary on the day's matches. His chemistry with the panel of pundits, including Frank McLintock, Chris Kamara, Rodney Marsh, and George Best, became the stuff of legend, fostering a sense of camaraderie and camaraderie among fans tuning in from home.

One of the key factors behind Soccer Saturday's enduring popularity was Stelling himself. His infectious enthusiasm, quick wit, and genuine love for the game resonated with viewers of all ages, making him a beloved figure in living rooms across the country. Whether celebrating a last-minute winner or commiserating a shocking upset, Stelling's emotional investment in every moment endeared him to fans and cemented his place as an iconic presence in British sports broadcasting.

In addition to his role on Soccer Saturday, Stelling also made waves as the host of Monday Night Football, further solidifying his reputation as one of Sky Sports' most versatile and beloved presenters. While his tenure coincided with a new format for the show, Stelling's charisma and passion for the game remained constant, earning him praise from viewers and pundits alike.

In the following chapters, we will explore Stelling's impact on Soccer Saturday in greater detail, examining the factors that contributed to its unparalleled success and the enduring legacy of one of British television's most beloved programs. From his legendary catchphrases to his heartfelt tributes to the beautiful game, Robert Jeffrey Stelling's Sky Sports career is a testament to the power of passion, dedication, and the ability to connect with audiences on a profound level.

Chapter 4: Expansion into Game Shows

Robert Jeffrey Stelling's illustrious broadcasting career extended beyond the realm of sports, showcasing his versatility and charm as a presenter in various entertainment formats. His foray into hosting game shows marked a new chapter in his journey, allowing him to showcase his wit, intellect, and magnetic personality to a broader audience.

One of Stelling's notable ventures into the world of game shows was his role as the host of Countdown, a popular British quiz show known for its blend of wordplay and mathematical challenges. Taking the helm in 2009, Stelling brought his trademark energy and enthusiasm to the iconic program, injecting new life into the beloved format. His rapport with contestants and skillful navigation of the show's challenges endeared him to audiences, earning praise for his engaging and charismatic hosting style.

Stelling's tenure on Countdown showcased his versatility as a presenter, proving that his talents extended far beyond the realm of sports broadcasting. His ability to command the stage with confidence and humor made him a natural fit for the role, further solidifying his status as one of Britain's most beloved television personalities.

In addition to Countdown, Stelling also showcased his hosting prowess on Alphabetical, a daytime game show that premiered on ITV in 2016. The show, which tested contestants' knowledge of the alphabet in a series of word-based challenges, provided Stelling with another opportunity to shine in the world of entertainment. His affable demeanor and quick wit endeared him to viewers, making Alphabetical a hit among audiences of all ages.

Stelling's success as a game show host underscored his versatility and adaptability as a presenter, proving that he could excel in a variety of formats beyond sports broadcasting. Whether guiding contestants through complex word puzzles or delivering witty banter on the set of Countdown, Stelling's charm and charisma captivated audiences and cemented his status as a television icon.

In the following chapters, we will delve deeper into Stelling's diverse portfolio of television appearances, exploring his contributions to popular culture and his enduring impact on the world of entertainment. From his memorable cameos in TV series to his acclaimed hosting gigs on game shows, Robert Jeffrey Stelling's expansion into new frontiers is a testament to his talent, versatility, and enduring appeal.

Chapter 5: Notable Appearances and Radio Work

Robert Jeffrey Stelling's influence extends far beyond the realm of sports broadcasting, with notable appearances in television series and advertisements that have solidified his status as a beloved figure in popular culture. Additionally, his radio work has been instrumental in connecting with audiences on a more personal level, with his current role at Talksport's breakfast show serving as a testament to his enduring appeal and versatility.

Stelling's television appearances have spanned a wide range of genres, showcasing his ability to seamlessly transition between roles and captivate audiences with his wit and charm. One of his most notable appearances was in the football comedy TV series Ted Lasso, where he played himself, adding authenticity and humor to the show's narrative. His cameo roles in popular series such as The IT Crowd, Dream Team, and Mike Bassett: Manager further demonstrated his versatility as a performer and his ability to leave a lasting impression on audiences.

In addition to his television work, Stelling has also made waves in the world of advertising, with memorable appearances in commercials that have garnered attention and acclaim. Notably, his role in an advert for Sky Broadband in 2013 showcased his comedic timing and charisma, further enhancing his appeal as a recognizable and relatable personality in the advertising world.

Beyond his appearances in television series and advertisements, Stelling's radio work has been a cornerstone of his career, allowing him to connect with audiences on a more intimate level through his engaging and insightful commentary. His current role at Talksport's breakfast show, where he co-hosts alongside Ally McCoist, demonstrates his continued relevance and influence in the world of radio broadcasting. With his trademark wit and humor, Stelling continues to entertain and inform listeners, making Talksport's breakfast show a must-listen for sports enthusiasts and radio aficionados alike.

In the following chapters, we will explore Stelling's enduring impact on popular culture through his television appearances and advertising work, as well as his continued contributions to radio broadcasting. From his memorable cameos to his engaging radio commentary, Robert Jeffrey Stelling's wide-ranging influence reflects his status as a beloved and respected figure in the world of media and entertainment.

Chapter 5: Notable Appearances and Radio Work

Robert Jeffrey Stelling's charismatic presence extends beyond the sports arena, with notable appearances in television series and advertisements that have cemented his influence in popular culture. Additionally, his radio work has been a cornerstone of his career, allowing him to connect with audiences on a more intimate level and showcase his diverse talents.

Stelling's television appearances have spanned a variety of genres, demonstrating his versatility as a performer and his ability to engage audiences across different platforms. One of his standout roles was in the football comedy TV series Ted Lasso, where he made cameo appearances as himself. Stelling's appearances added authenticity and humor to the show, further endearing him to viewers and showcasing his knack for comedic timing.

In addition to his television roles, Stelling has also made memorable appearances in advertisements, leveraging his charm and charisma to connect with audiences in the commercial sphere. His role in an advert for Sky Broadband in 2013, where he spoofed a previous Sky Broadband advert starring Bruce Willis, highlighted his ability to inject humor and personality into advertising campaigns, further solidifying his status as a recognizable and relatable figure in popular culture.

Beyond his work in television and advertising, Stelling's radio career has been instrumental in establishing his connection with audiences and showcasing his talents as a broadcaster. His current role as a co-host on Talksport's breakfast show, alongside Ally McCoist, exemplifies his continued relevance and influence in the world of radio broadcasting. With his sharp wit, engaging banter, and deep knowledge of sports, Stelling entertains and informs listeners on a daily basis, making Talksport's breakfast show a must-listen for sports fans and radio enthusiasts alike.

In summary, Robert Jeffrey Stelling's impact on popular culture extends far beyond the sports arena, with notable appearances in television series and advertisements showcasing his wider influence. His radio work, including his current role at Talksport's breakfast show, further underscores his versatility and enduring appeal as a beloved figure in the world of media and entertainment.

Chapter 6: Honours and Recognition

Throughout his illustrious career, Robert Jeffrey Stelling has been the recipient of numerous honours and awards, recognizing his outstanding contributions to sports journalism and broadcasting. These accolades serve as a testament to his dedication, professionalism, and lasting impact on the industry.

One of the most notable honours bestowed upon Stelling is his honorary Doctor of Professional Studies, awarded by the University of Teesside on November 23, 2007. This prestigious recognition reflects Stelling's significant achievements in the field of broadcasting and his commitment to excellence in his craft. It acknowledges his influence as a respected figure in the world of media and his contributions to inspiring future generations of journalists and broadcasters.

In addition to his academic honours, Stelling was appointed a Member of the Order of the British Empire (MBE) in the 2024 New Year Honours for his services to sport, broadcasting, and charity. This prestigious honour recognizes Stelling's remarkable impact on the landscape of sports journalism and broadcasting, as well as his philanthropic efforts in support of charitable causes. It underscores his enduring commitment to using his platform for the greater good and making a positive difference in the lives of others.

Stelling's contributions to sports journalism and broadcasting have been nothing short of extraordinary. As the host of Gillette Soccer Saturday for nearly three decades, he played a pivotal role in shaping the way football is covered and celebrated on television. His passion for the game, encyclopedic knowledge, and engaging presenting style endeared him to millions of viewers, making Soccer Saturday a beloved institution and essential viewing for football fans across the country.

Beyond his role on Soccer Saturday, Stelling's impact on sports broadcasting extends to his coverage of other sporting events, including his tenure as the main presenter of Sky's live Champions League coverage. His insightful commentary, professionalism, and ability to capture the excitement of live sporting moments have earned him widespread acclaim and cemented his status as one of the most respected voices in the industry.

In summary, Robert Jeffrey Stelling's honours and recognition underscore the profound impact he has had on sports journalism and broadcasting throughout his career. From his honorary Doctorate to his appointment as an MBE, these accolades reflect his unwavering dedication to his craft and his enduring legacy as a trailblazer in the field. Stelling's contributions to the industry have left an indelible mark, inspiring generations of broadcasters and earning him a rightful place among the most esteemed figures in British media.

Chapter 7: Personal Life and Charity Work

Beyond the glitz and glamour of the broadcasting world, Robert Jeffrey Stelling leads a rich and fulfilling personal life centered around family, hobbies, and a deep commitment to philanthropy. His dedication to making a positive impact extends far beyond the confines of the television screen, as he actively engages in charitable endeavors and gives back to his community in meaningful ways.

Stelling's family plays a central role in his life, providing him with love, support, and a sense of grounding amid the demands of his career. He resides in Bishop's Waltham, Hampshire, with his wife Liz and their three children: sons Robbie and Matthew, and daughter Olivia. Their close-knit family unit serves as a source of strength and inspiration, grounding Stelling in what truly matters amidst the hustle and bustle of his professional endeavors.

In addition to his familial responsibilities, Stelling nurtures a variety of hobbies and interests outside of broadcasting. He is an avid runner, having completed the London Marathon on eight occasions, with his personal best time standing at an impressive 3 hours and 28 minutes. Stelling's passion for running not only serves as a means of physical fitness but also as a source of personal fulfillment and accomplishment.

Stelling's philanthropic efforts are perhaps most notably exemplified by his involvement in charity walks and fundraising initiatives, particularly in support of Prostate Cancer UK. In 2016, he embarked on a monumental journey, walking 262 miles from Hartlepool United to Wembley Stadium over the course of 10 days. The walk, which raised over £420,000 for Prostate Cancer UK, captured the hearts and minds of supporters nationwide, showcasing Stelling's unwavering commitment to raising awareness and funds for a cause close to his heart.

This remarkable feat of endurance and generosity was not an isolated endeavor for Stelling, who has continued to pledge his support to Prostate Cancer UK through various fundraising initiatives in the years that followed. His dedication to raising awareness about the disease and supporting those affected by it underscores his compassionate nature and his belief in using his platform for the greater good.

In summary, Robert Jeffrey Stelling's personal life and charity work offer a glimpse into the man behind the microphone—a devoted husband, father, and philanthropist with a passion for making a difference in the world. His commitment to family, hobbies, and charitable endeavors speaks volumes about his character and values, solidifying his legacy as not only a respected broadcaster but also a compassionate and generous individual dedicated to serving others.

Chapter 8: Challenges and Triumphs

Robert Jeffrey Stelling's illustrious career has been marked by both triumphs and challenges, including a notable instance of personal adversity detailed in his book. Despite facing obstacles along the way, Stelling's resilience, determination, and unwavering passion for his craft have enabled him to overcome adversity and emerge stronger than ever.

One of the most significant challenges Stelling faced in his career was a blackmail attempt detailed in his book, "I've Got Mail." In the book, Stelling revealed that he had been targeted by scammers who sent letters to his home demanding a £50,000 payment in exchange for keeping false accusations of sexual assault quiet. This distressing experience undoubtedly posed a significant threat to Stelling's personal and professional reputation, causing immense stress and anxiety for him and his family.

However, Stelling's response to this adversity speaks volumes about his character and resilience. Rather than succumbing to fear or allowing himself to be silenced, he chose to confront the situation head-on, seeking support from his wife and leveraging his connections to uncover the truth behind the scam. By sharing his story openly and honestly in his book and subsequent radio interviews, Stelling not only exposed the perpetrators but also demonstrated his courage and determination in the face of adversity.

In addition to this personal challenge, Stelling has undoubtedly encountered professional obstacles throughout his career, including the pressures of live broadcasting, the demands of a highly competitive industry, and the inevitable scrutiny that comes with being in the public eye. Yet, time and time again, he has risen to the occasion, delivering stellar performances and earning the respect and admiration of colleagues and audiences alike.

Stelling's ability to overcome challenges and thrive in his profession can be attributed to several key factors, including his passion for his craft, his dedication to continuous improvement, and his ability to maintain perspective in the face of adversity. Whether navigating the fast-paced world of live television or confronting personal challenges head-on, Stelling's resilience and determination have been the driving forces behind his success.

In summary, Robert Jeffrey Stelling's career has been punctuated by both triumphs and challenges, including a notable instance of personal adversity detailed in his book. However, his resilience, courage, and unwavering commitment to his craft have enabled him to overcome obstacles and emerge stronger than ever. Stelling's ability to confront challenges head-on and continue thriving in his profession serves as a testament to his character and his enduring legacy as one of Britain's most beloved broadcasters.

Chapter 9: Legacy and Impact

Robert Jeffrey Stelling's legacy in the world of sports broadcasting and entertainment is nothing short of profound, leaving an indelible mark on the industry and inspiring future generations of broadcasters. Throughout his illustrious career, Stelling has captivated audiences with his wit, charm, and encyclopedic knowledge of the game, earning him a rightful place among the most esteemed figures in British media.

One of Stelling's most enduring contributions to the industry is his iconic tenure as the host of Gillette Soccer Saturday, a beloved institution that has become essential viewing for football fans across the country. For nearly three decades, Stelling guided viewers through the highs and lows of the football season, providing live updates, analysis, and commentary on the day's matches. His infectious enthusiasm, quick wit, and genuine love for the game endeared him to millions of viewers, making Soccer Saturday a cultural phenomenon and a cherished part of British sporting heritage.

Beyond Soccer Saturday, Stelling's influence extends to his coverage of other sporting events, including his role as the main presenter of Sky's live Champions League coverage. His insightful commentary, professionalism, and ability to capture the excitement of live sporting moments have earned him widespread acclaim and cemented his status as one of the most respected voices in the industry.

Moreover, Stelling's versatility as a broadcaster has inspired countless aspiring journalists and broadcasters, demonstrating that success in the field requires not only talent but also passion, dedication, and a relentless pursuit of excellence. His ability to connect with audiences on a personal level, coupled with his unwavering commitment to delivering top-notch coverage, has set a standard of excellence for future generations to aspire to.

Stelling's lasting impact on the industry is perhaps best reflected in the admiration and respect he commands from colleagues, viewers, and fans alike. His legendary catchphrases, memorable moments, and unparalleled professionalism have left an indelible imprint on British media, shaping the way sports broadcasting is perceived and celebrated.

In conclusion, Robert Jeffrey Stelling's legacy in the world of sports broadcasting and entertainment is one of enduring significance and influence. His contributions to the industry, from his iconic tenure on Soccer Saturday to his role as a mentor and inspiration to future broadcasters, have solidified his status as a beloved and respected figure in British media. As his career continues to inspire and entertain audiences, Stelling's legacy will undoubtedly endure for generations to come, ensuring that his impact on the industry remains etched in the annals of broadcasting history.

Chapter 10: Conclusion

Robert Jeffrey Stelling's journey through the world of sports broadcasting is a testament to the power of passion, perseverance, and unwavering dedication. From his humble beginnings as a journalist at the Hartlepool Mail to his iconic tenure as the host of Gillette Soccer Saturday, Stelling has carved out a legendary career defined by his infectious enthusiasm, quick wit, and genuine love for the game.

Throughout his career, Stelling has not only entertained millions of viewers with his engaging commentary and insightful analysis but has also inspired future generations of broadcasters with his professionalism and commitment to excellence. His impact on the industry extends far beyond the confines of the television screen, as he has used his platform to raise awareness for charitable causes and make a positive difference in the lives of others.

Despite facing challenges along the way, including a notable instance of personal adversity detailed in his book, Stelling has emerged stronger than ever, proving that resilience and determination are the keys to overcoming obstacles and achieving success. His legacy in the world of sports broadcasting is one of enduring significance and influence, as his contributions continue to shape the way sports are covered and celebrated on television.

As we reflect on Stelling's remarkable journey and contributions, we are reminded of the profound impact one individual can have on an entire industry. His passion, professionalism, and unwavering dedication serve as an inspiration to us all, reminding us to pursue our dreams with vigor and to always strive for excellence in everything we do.

In the end, Robert Jeffrey Stelling's legacy will endure as a shining example of what it means to leave a lasting imprint on the world, not only through his accomplishments in broadcasting but also through his compassion, generosity, and commitment to making a positive difference. As we bid farewell to one of Britain's most beloved broadcasters, we are left with the enduring reminder that true greatness lies not only in what we achieve but in how we touch the lives of others along the way.

Printed in Great Britain
by Amazon